# Morning
# and
# Evening
# *Prayers*

Publications International, Ltd.

# Table of Contents

January

# *Evening*

Father, the beginning of a new year speaks of a fresh start and new opportunities. It is a good time to teach our children about forgiveness and trying again when we have failed.

We are thankful that you are a God of second chances. Just as you love us unconditionally, there is nothing our children could do to make us stop loving them. Help us teach them the hopeful message that there is no need for despair; that forgiveness and a new start are always possible.

# Morning

The calendar is as bare as the Christmas tree, the page of tomorrow clean and ready. May God bless the New Year that beckons, helping us face what we must, celebrate every triumph we can, and make the changes we need. And now celebrate to the fullest this whistle-blowing, toast raising moment, for it is the threshold between the old and new us.

# Evening

For the promise you unfold with the opening of each day, I thank you, Lord.

For blessings shared along the way, I thank you, Lord.

For the comfort of our home filled with love to keep us warm, I thank you, Lord.

For shelter from the winter storm, I thank you, Lord.

For the gifts of peace and grace you grant the family snug within, I thank you, Lord.

For shielding us from harm and sin, I thank you, Lord.

For the beauty of the snow sparkling in the winter sun, I thank you, Lord.

For the peace when the day is done, I thank you, Lord.

# Morning

Dear God, I long to change parts of my life that are no longer working, but don't know where to start. Help me break down these big, scary goals into small and achievable steps. Give me courage to put these plans into action and turn my life around!

# Evening

As for God, his way is perfect: the word of the Lord is tried: he is a buckler to all those that trust in him.

—Psalm 18:30

# Morning

Give me a hint, steadfast God, about what lies ahead, for I want to see around the corner to the future. If that's not possible, help me live as if the future is now, assured that each day's grace will be sufficient.

# Evening

Sidetracked, lost, and wandering far from the home of the heart, I long to be at home with you. Home, not so much a place as a togetherness where I am loved and welcomed just as I am, where I am sheltered, nourished, equipped, and sent on my way. And to where, when I stray, I will be found and returned. I get a glimpse of being at home with you, God, when I discover I am being constantly nurtured by an ever-present Parent.

# Morning

For a day in thy courts is better than a thousand. I had rather be a doorkeeper in the house of my God, than to dwell in the tents of wickedness.

—Psalm 84:10

# Evening

He giveth snow like wool: he scattereth the
hoarfrost like ashes.

—Psalm 147:16

# Morning

Bless us, Lord, as we go to worship this morning. Look down upon our efforts to honor your name through song and word and fellowship. And help us do it. For only in your power do we live and move. And in your being alone we find our true identity.

# *Evening*

From the rising of the sun unto the going down of the same the Lord's name is to be praised.

—Psalm 113:3

# Morning

So many things will offer themselves to me for "worship" today. But reveal yourself, God, in all your creativity, as the only being worthy of my true adoration.

# Evening

Our worries are hard to dismiss, Lord. They seem to grow bigger and bigger until they take over our lives. Please help us conquer them, one at a time. Your reassurance is welcome. Amen.

# Morning

We are blinded by our sorrow. Lift our eyes and bless us, O Father, with a defiant hope, steadfast trust, and fire in the belly to emerge from this darkness victorious and whole once again, standing in the light you've given us.

# Evening

We want to belong and go to great lengths to fit anonymously in, forgetting we are like snowflakes, no two, thank God, alike. Each snowflake and child of yours is the same in essence but different in form. Bless our unique, one-of-a-kind value. We are heartened to know that no one is created more special. It is not your way to make one snowflake, or one person, better than another.

# Morning

I have called upon thee, for thou wilt hear me, O God: incline thine ear unto me, and hear my speech.

—Psalm 17:6

# Evening

I am feeling my way in this darkness, God, and it seems I'm going in circles. Yet you have reminded me—quietly, just now—that I am encircled by your love. Wherever I go, whatever direction, I am already centered in your all-encompassing love.

# Morning

Lord, thank you for being a God of new beginnings. Give me a fresh start today as I trust in you. Amen.

# Evening

Create in me a clean heart, O God; and
renew a right spirit within me.

—Psalm 51:10

# Morning

Lord, how it must amuse you at times to see us orchestrating the details of our days as if everything and everyone were in our control. It's only when you are involved in our plans that things go smoothly, Lord. Teach us to trust that your way is the better way, even when we can't see how every detail will turn out. Our insight is only as good as our reliance on you. Please be with us each day, Lord.

# Evening

God, I know that you close some doors in my life in order to open new ones. I know that things change and come to an end in order to leave room for new beginnings. Help me have the boldness and enthusiasm to let go of the old and accept the new. Amen.

# Morning

In the dead of winter, God of springtimes, I'm gardening. Carrot tops rooting, sweet potatoes vining. I don't doubt the outcome since I've learned at your knee to live as if. As if useless can become useful; as if seemingly dead can live; as if spring will come.

With Solomon, I will rejoice. Winter will pass. Flowers will appear in the land. The season of singing will come.

How does a winter garden grow? With hope. It grows brighter each time I live as if, knowing that you, O God, color even our wintry days from love's spring palette.

# *Evening*

Turn thee unto me, and have mercy upon me; for I am desolate and afflicted. The troubles of my heart are enlarged: O bring thou me out of my distresses.
—Psalm 25:16–17

# Morning

I know yours is a persistent devotion, Lord.
Your devoted love for me is the example that
helps me to love others as well. What would
I prefer to your love? What could I love more
than those I hold dear? Nothing in the universe!
Who are the loves of my life? Let me count them
all and delight in them today.

# Evening

In silence I kneel in your presence—bow my heart to your wisdom; lift my hands for your mercy. And open my soul to the great gift: I am already held in your arms.

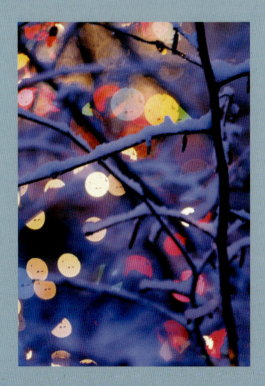

# Morning

As I work on my outward appearance each morning, help me to remember that my inner person needs attention too—especially since that's what you focus on. Your evaluation of my heart is far more important to me than any single human opinion about my appearance or fashion sense.

# *Evening*

Be merciful unto me, O God, be merciful unto
me: for my soul trusteth in thee: yea, in the
shadow of thy wings will I make my refuge,
until these calamities be overpast.

—Psalm 57:1

# Morning

Father, your Word makes it clear to me that the life of faith is not passive. While we wait for you to answer prayer, grant wisdom, and open doors, we also keep our minds sharp and our hearts strengthened by reading and studying your Word, by meeting with you in prayer, and by finding encouragement among other believers. These are the disciplines our souls need to stay focused on ever-present hope.

# Evening

Lord, today a white lie slipped out of my mouth
to save me from a trying commitment. As soon
as I felt your little tug on my conscience, I knew
I had to come clean about it and repair my
relationship with you and with my friend.

I know that the lie wasn't small in your eyes,
and it was a reminder to me that I am always
vulnerable to sin. If I didn't feel your nudge
to repair the situation as quickly as possible,
I might have fallen into a complacency that
would make me vulnerable to any number of
more serious sins. I thank you for nudging me,
Lord, and for forgiving me, yet again.

# Morning

Lord, sometimes I long to stand out. I notice others with shinier hair, amazing figures, and impeccable outfits, and I feel so plain. At these times, help me to remember that I should be at work cultivating the gentle and quiet spirit that is precious to you. This type of spirit may not call out, "Here I am!" but over the long run, it accomplishes much. I am doing what I can, and I leave the rest to you. I trust that you will bring all to fruition.

# Evening

Happy is that people, that is in such a case: yea, happy is that people, whose God is the Lord.

—Psalm 144:15

# Morning

Lord, how much time do we spend looking into a mirror, and how often do we see you there? We were made in your image, but rather than focusing on that, we often focus on all the things we'd like to change. When others look at us, do they see our meager attempts to make our lips fuller and our eyelashes longer, or do they see the light of your love shining through our eyes? Teach us to focus less on our own appearance and concentrate more on presenting your face to those around us. It is you the world needs, not us.

# Evening

Lord, help me not accuse you of being untrue when I don't get from you everything I want, for you have promised to meet all my needs. And when I learn to love you supremely and trust you wholly, my desires will find fulfillment in you.

February

# Evening

Thou wilt shew me the path of life: in thy presence is fulness of joy; at thy right hand there are pleasures for evermore.

—Psalm 16:11

# Morning

Sometimes it is difficult to appreciate snowy weather, but I thank God for the gift of snow days. How wonderful it is for everyone to be home, safe and warm. On snow days, life returns to a simpler pace and the demands of schedules and responsibilities fall away. Thank you, Lord, for the beauty of the snow and the time it gives us to relax and share quiet times with our loved ones.

# Evening

O give thanks unto the Lord; for he is good:
because his mercy endureth for ever.

—Psalm 118:1

# Morning

Winters can be long, Lord, as I've complained before, and hope elusive. Thank you for sending me outdoors. My spirit soars at the sight of a woodchuck waking from winter sleep. I rub sleep from my eyes, grateful for signposts of change, like pawprints in the mud, leading me to springs of the soul.

# Evening

When I think about your example of love, dear God, I realize that love is far more than a warm emotion. It is a deep commitment to look out for another's best interest, even at my own expense. Please teach me to put my pride and my heart on the line. Please protect me, Lord, as I love others in your name. Amen.

# Morning

What a blessing to have a second chance! Grant me the wisdom to use this opportunity wisely. And save me from the fear that I'll fall into the same old traps as last time. This is a brand new day, a whole new beginning.

# Evening

Lord, we want to live life to its fullest. And although we know we shouldn't place our own wants before others' wants, it is so easy to think our dreams for the future matter most. Remind us to make compromises. Our love can get us further in this life than selfishness. Amen.

# Morning

Good morning, God! We greet you with our many morning faces. We arise sometimes grumpy, sometimes smiling, sometimes prepared, sometimes behind. Always may we turn to you first in our family prayer. Bless us today and join us in it.

# Evening

The day is thine, the night also is thine: thou hast prepared the light and the sun. Thou hast set all the borders of the earth: thou hast made summer and winter.

—Psalm 74:16–17

# Morning

God, it's a quiet day. Help me pause to listen to you, to talk to you, to enjoy your company. Chase away my guilt and shame and fear, and draw me close to your heart. Remind me that no matter what my earthly roles may be, in your presence I am your child, and you care for me more than I could ever imagine. Let me lean against your heart now, Father, and hear it beating with love for me. Amen.

# Evening

Today I am tired, Lord. There seem to be too many things on my to-do list and too few hours in the day. And still, I know what a blessing it is to have work to do and to live a purpose-filled life. Thank you for tasks large and small that give meaning to our days, Lord. May we always do each one as if we were doing it only for you. And may we never assume we can do anything without your direction and energy.

# Morning

Lord, how I pray that your love is evident in me today! I want to follow you closely and help draw others to you as well. I know that if those with whom I come in contact see love, joy, peace, patience, kindness, goodness, faithfulness, gentleness, and self-control in me, they may find you as well. Direct my steps as I follow you, Lord, and may the grace you've sprinkled on me be revealed for your glory. Amen.

# Evening

Lord God, why is it that we tend to hold so tightly to the things of this world? We know in our hearts that everything we have is ours only by your grace and great generosity. When we accumulate more than we need, it only builds barriers between ourselves and you. Thank you for your provision, Lord. May we learn to hold everything loosely, knowing it is only borrowed.

# Morning

Lord, this is one of those days when I really don't know which way to turn. I've lost my sense of direction and feel as if I'm sitting on a rock in the forest, wondering which trail will take me back to familiar ground. Lead me, Lord. Send the signs I need to follow to get where you want me to go. I put my trust in you.

# Evening

Let my prayer be set forth before thee as incense; and the lifting up of my hands as the evening sacrifice.

—Psalm 141:2

# Morning

Keep us from being beholden to time, Lord. You always create time and space for anything we are doing that brings you glory. Teach us to rest in the knowledge that time is in your hands. Whenever we think we don't have enough of it, show us you have plenty and are happy to share! Thank you, Lord, for your generous supply of time.

# *Evening*

O Lord, your gift of love is often distorted in this world of ours. You are the source of the only perfect love we will ever know. Thank you, Lord, for abiding in us and helping us love ourselves and others. On this day, Lord, I pray that you will draw near to anyone who is feeling unloved. May they accept your unconditional love so they will know what true love is!

# Morning

It's amazing, steadfast God, how much better I feel after sharing with you even the smallest doubt or little niggling worry about being the best I can be. Connected, we can do great things. Alone, I am the victim of my own fears.

# Evening

My days are like a shadow that declineth; and I am withered like grass. But thou, O Lord, shall endure for ever; and thy remembrance unto all generations.

—Psalm 102:11–12

# Morning

Help me to see with new eyes today—especially the burden of care that others harbor within them. Grant me insight to see beyond smiling faces into hearts that hurt. And when I recognize the pain, Lord, let me reach out.

# Evening

Your Word fills my heart with hope, Lord.
Sometimes—when I'm lost on this path of
life—I sense your presence. It is so comforting
to think of you searching tirelessly to find me
again. Grant me your grace so I can stay on
your path more steadily. This way, you'll have
more time to devote to searching out others!

# Morning

How can I be pure in heart, Lord? I certainly don't always have right thoughts and motives. Perhaps being pure in heart can happen through being honest about what's going on inside my heart and working to purify it. I can make it a point to focus on what is right and true and good, continually turning my heart toward you to find those things and be renewed in them. That's why I'm here right now, Lord. Purify my heart as I walk close to you today and enjoy the blessing of fellowship with you.

# *Evening*

Sometimes it's good to just step back and look at the whole picture of who you are, Lord—to remember your greatness. When I look at how big you are, my problems that seemed so gigantic a few moments ago seem silly. My big plans seem less important, and my high notions of myself get cut down to size. I come away not feeling diminished, but rather lifted up in spirit and full of faith. We were made to praise you!

# Morning

Lord, teach me how to help and defend the vulnerable people around me—the children, the sick, the infirm, the elderly, the poor. They are easily taken advantage of by those more powerful than they are, but I know you have a special place in your heart for them. Help me not to look the other way when intervening would be inconvenient or scary. Grant me your wisdom, insight, and grace to effectively help wherever and whenever I can.

# Evening

The Lord is on my side; I will not
fear: what can man do unto me?
—Psalm 118:6

# Morning

Lord, what comfort we find in your changeless nature. When we look back and remember all the ways you've guided us in the past, we know we have no need to be anxious about the future. You were, are, and always will be our Savior and Lord. Why should we fear instability when you are always here with us?

# Evening

Lord, in my darkest moments, it is easy to despair and fear that you have given up on me. It would be understandable for you to be angry and disappointed and leave me to my ruin. How comforting it is to know that the minute I regret what I have done and turn to you, you are right where you have been all along—by my side, ready to embrace and carry me until I am strong enough to take a step on my own. Thank you for your faithfulness, Lord—especially when I least deserve it.

# Morning

I have such good intentions, Lord of promise, but sometimes I slip in carrying them out. Guide my actions so that they match my words as I make footprints for my children to follow. Make me worthy of being a pathfinder. Amen.

# *Evening*

Thank you for the difficult people in my life. They show me that not everything can be easy. When I try to connect with someone who is hard to get along with or who doesn't agree with me, I think of how Jesus reached out even to those who did not agree with him. Allow me to be like Jesus and be thankful for the opportunity to extend my heart to everyone.

# Morning

Thank you for my community. As I run my errands and conduct my business, let me remember to be grateful for everyone who helps me. From a clerk at the store to the police officer keeping me safe, my community is filled with people who help others. Thank you, Lord, for putting these people in my life and for giving me the chance to know them. May I always work to make my community a better place.

# Evening

The Lord redeemeth the soul of his servants: and none of them that trust in him shall be desolate.

—Psalm 34:22

March

# *Evening*

Today my mind is thinking of places far away from me. I am grateful for the places I have traveled to and the opportunity to see new things and meet new people. I am grateful for the places I haven't seen and the anticipation and promise of trips to come. Thank you, Lord, for making it possible for me to leave my surroundings and visit new places.

# Morning

Loving God, help us sense your angelic messengers whenever and wherever and however they come to us. In the darkness of winter, the brightness of spring, the abundance of summer, the transitions of autumn, may we expect to be visited by your heavenly beings. And when those visits happen, may our eyes be open and our gratitude heartfelt.

# Evening

Father God, in you I find comfort and peace after a day of working hard and pushing forward to reach my goals. In you I find strength when I've done all I can do on my own. In you I find my spirit renewed. Amen.

# Morning

Daily stresses disorient me as completely as a red-winged blackbird, herald of spring, lost in an unexpected snow. I am found, Lord, when I see your fingerprint in the whorls of a fern unfurling, lacy green and bold in the snow, and know that you are in charge and endure, that you persevere and I, in you, can too. Then I know I was never lost at all, just a bit off-course like a surprised bird.

# Evening

Lord, sometimes I get frustrated, especially when I have to face something new. Thank you for giving me an open heart. Help me accept change and rejoice in new experiences and new people. Help me to be grateful for new opportunities and always see the good things even when I am afraid to try something new.

# Morning

Thank you for the funny bone, Lord, placed next to hearts broken by anxiety and fear. A good belly laugh is a gift from you, expanding and healing heart, lungs, and mind.

# *Evening*

God, I ask for a bold and courageous faith to get me through these trials and tribulations. Let me stand on my own feet, but steady my footing with the knowledge of your presence. Give me the strength of will to never give up, no matter how crazy life gets.

# Morning

I come to church today, not because of duty or because a preacher calls, but because you, O God, invite me, your child, for whom you've been searching. In the words and songs, the lights and symbols, I feel, like a pulse, your spirit beating within me.

# Evening

The Lord will strengthen him upon the bed of languishing: thou wilt make all his bed in his sickness.

—Psalm 41:3

# Morning

I am grateful, God of Hope, for the gift of each new day, each new season, like the one unfolding around me now in flower and birdsong, in seedling and bud. When they arrive as surely as dawn follows night and bloom follows bulb, I am uplifted by the fulfillment of your promise.

# Evening

Lord, it's so easy for us to get bogged down in the details of life on this earth. But when we have the opportunity to gaze up at the stars on a clear night, it is easy to remember that there is so much more to your creation than our relatively insignificant lives. You placed the stars and know them by name, Lord, and you know us by name too. We are blessed to be even a tiny part of your magnificent creation! That you also care so deeply for us is the best gift of all.

# Morning

Lord, sometimes I feel you've blessed me with all kinds of knowledge that no one is interested in hearing! Help me know when and how to share your wisdom with others. Help me to show others your truth, rather than just talk about it. You taught us by living out the truth, Lord. Help us to do the same.

# *Evening*

Good friends make us better people by keeping us sharp. If we allow our friends to challenge our perspective, discuss the meaningful stuff of life, and keep us accountable to what is true and right and good, we understand the value of being sharpened. And if we're willing to reciprocate—sometimes even at the risk of hurting our friend out of a heart of love for them—then we understand the value of being good sharpeners. It's true that this sharpening process isn't always pleasant, but it's always good. True friends embrace this reality.

# Morning

Lord, how hopelessly aware we are of our earthly bodies. They develop creaks and frailties—not to mention weird bumps and lumps! But thanks to you, we are so much more than our bodies. For although we live in the flesh, we are filled with your Holy Spirit; the life we live is really you living out your life in us! Thank you for that perspective, Lord. It makes it so much easier to watch our earthly bodies begin to fail. How ready we will be to exchange them for the heavenly models!

# Evening

Lord, how good have you been to me? Let me count the ways! In times of discouragement all I need to do is sit quietly and remember all the times in the past when you stepped in to set wrongs right, gave me a second chance, or showed up with a last-minute miracle. Lord, you are so good. May my faith never waver in view of all the wonders you have wrought!

# Morning

Search me, O God, and know my heart: try me, and
know my thoughts: And see if there be any wicked
way in me, and lead me in the way everlasting.

—Psalm 139:23–24

# Evening

Whate'er my fears or foes suggest,
you are my hope, my joy, my rest.
My heart shall feel your love and raise
my cheerful voice to sing your praise.

—Isaac Watts

# Morning

Lord, today I ask you to slow me down and open my ears so I will notice the needs of those around me. Too often I breeze by people with an offhand greeting but remain in a cocoon of my own concerns. I know many around me are hurting, Lord. Help me find ways to be of service.

# *Evening*

Despite today's valley of shadow and sickness, I know you, shepherd of my soul, will continue restoring me as I move through treatment to the safe meadow of wellness.

# Morning

The Lord is my strength and song,
and is become my salvation

—Psalm 118:14

# Evening

Lord above, you look down upon us, and still you love us. When we look down on others, it is because we are angered and cannot see their points of view. We also still love them, but sometimes our anger clouds our love. Please help us stay grounded and find understanding. Amen.

# Morning

Calm me enough, O Lord, to breathe deeply and restoratively despite my racing heart, pounding headache, and generally fatigued body and mind. Prayer restores me in the presence of all that threatens to undo me, which I name to you now.

# Evening

Father God, the land is asleep. The buds of spring lie in wait. The wonder of your world seems in a holding pattern just waiting for the go-ahead to grow. Let winter teach us the value of stillness, of silence, and of meditation. Help us know that the angel wings don't have to flutter wildly to do the work of your kingdom of peace.

# Morning

Keep us connected, O God of all time, to those who've come before. Inspire us to tell family tales and to pull out family albums and family Bibles and handed-down antiques to show the connecting links of which your love forges us into a whole.

# Evening

It's late at night, and still there is much to do. Yet there is peace, holding onto childlike trust that God is an ever-present companion, showing us how not to burn out needlessly, worrying the candle at both ends.

# Morning

May He support us all the day long, till the shades lengthen, and the evening comes, and the busy world is hushed, and the fever of life is over, and our work is done! Then in His mercy may He give us a safe lodging, and a holy rest, and peace at the last.

—John Henry Newman

# Evening

Dear Lord, each night the news is full of trouble. So much pain and sorrow. It makes me ache to see it all. Some nights, it seems that's all there is; this world seems sometimes so weary and heavy laden. Then I turn to you and know that you are nearest on the darkest days. And there is comfort in knowing you and that you have not forsaken us or the people whose world is presently dark.

# Morning

Lord, it often happens that you are trying to communicate an important truth to us, but we are so busy searching for the truth elsewhere that we don't stop and listen. Teach us the importance of being still, Lord. Only when we are still can we be aware of your presence and hear your voice. Only when we quiet the stirrings of our own souls can we connect with your will! Speak to us, Lord—and help us be ready to listen.

# Evening

Creator God, you have come to me with healing in your hand. When I cried out, you heard me. You provided me with a gift that brought both peace and pleasure to my harried life. You helped me to focus on life instead of illness and sorrow. Lord, thank you for this wondrous gift. Amen.

# Morning

We are celebrating today, O God, a mixture of bunnies hiding colored eggs and angels rolling away stones. Join us as we gather to share a meal and ponder both, enjoying the one and giving thanks for the other. Bless those at this table savoring the food and the message of this day. Remind us, too, Lord of unexpected appearances, that this also is the season of spring, a time when rebirth is not so surprising after all. Send us after lunch into the yard where, hiding colored Easter eggs for the children, we may understand anew what this day really means.

# Evening

God of springtime surprises, bring back to life
friendships faded because of hurt feelings,
marriages broken from deceit, love crushed by
meanness. In the doing, hope glimmers like dawn's
first sun ray and thaws even the most frozen heart.

April

# Evening

Lord God, I kneel before you, and you alone.
I'm sorry for the times I've mistakenly
Credited someone else or something else
For your miraculous work.
How could an angel, a preacher, a friend
Impart your healing power, unless
You were behind it all,
Inspiring, instructing, empowering?
I thank you for the ones you use
On this earth and in your heaven
To help me heal.
Lord God, I kneel before you, and you alone.
Amen.

# Morning

After a long winter, the first day of warmer temperatures is a gift. We open the windows and though they first creak from disuse, soon fresh air enlivens the room. Our hearts quicken at the green scents of spring, at the promise of a new season and all the chapters yet to come. Opening our windows to a new time of year, we open our hearts and spirits.

# Evening

We plow the fields and scatter
The good seed on the land,
But it is fed and watered
By God's almighty hand;
He sends the snow in winter,
The warmth to swell the grain,
The breezes and the sunshine,
And soft, refreshing rain.
All good gifts around us
Are sent from heaven above:
Then thank the Lord, O thank the Lord
For all His love.

—Matthias Claudius

# Morning

Dear God, I rise each day in the power of your love, knowing I can accomplish anything. I rise each day in joy, feeling your will move through me, knowing I can achieve all things.

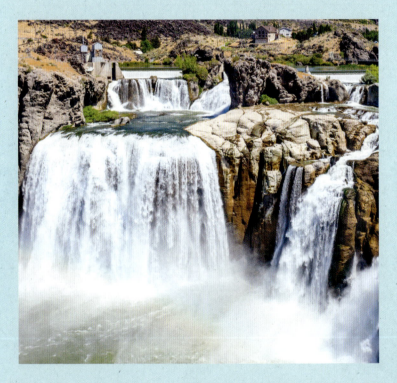

# Evening

What a blessing, Almighty One, to be able to earn a living for the family! To be free of worry about what they will eat or wear. You have given us so much: house, flowers, table and chairs, beds, and blankets. And your gifts are a serious calling: Show us how to give in return!

# Morning

God, you are so great. It is always the right time to worship you, but morning is best. Praise for the dawning light that streams in through this window. Praise for the sound of the birds as they flit through in the air. Praise for the little spider crawling along on the ceiling. Praise for the smell of coffee and the warmth of a cup in my hands. Praise for the flowering plants—and even those weeds growing by the house. Praise for the neighbors walking along the sidewalk and the clouds moving by, too. Most of all, praise for the breath that keeps flowing in and out of my lungs. Yes, this is the greatest item of praise: that you alone are my life—all life itself. Without you, all is dust. Praise . . . for you.

# Evening

Time is tight, Lord, and I wonder why I bother to pray. The question is answer enough: I need a relationship where I don't have to bluff and hurry. And when I pray boldly? I offer myself as a possible answer to prayer. No time to waste.

# Morning

Dear God, we trust you to show us joy when the time comes. We know that good follows bad. Please help us be patient. Amen.

# Evening

Comfort me in my day of need with a love that is infinite and true. Ignore my lack of desire to forgive and forget. Fill my anger with the waters of peace and serenity that I may come to accept this situation and move on to a greater level of understanding and knowing.

# Morning

What a relief in this throwaway world of ever-changing values to know that you, God, are the same yesterday, today, and tomorrow. Your trustworthiness and desire for all your children to have good things never varies. You are as sure as sunrise and sunset.

# Evening

Although the rain still falls, Creator God,
it takes such a little bit of sun to create a
rainbow, your sign of promise and presence.

# Morning

How fortunate I feel today!
All is well.
Things are working out.
But is it luck . . . or is it your love?
I will assume the latter
and offer words of praise:
Bless your name, Almighty One!

# Evening

God gave the rainbow as a sign of his promise to never flood the entire earth again. The colors that spread out in spectrum, as sunlight passes through water droplets in the sky, speak of God's faithfulness in keeping his promise to Noah and to all the generations that have followed. Faithfulness marks God's character. It is who he is, through and through. Let every rainbow we see remind us of God's faithful love, and let praise flow from our hearts to the one who always keeps his promises.

# *Morning*

I do sometimes prefer frivolity and flattery to growing in the light of some uncomfortable truth, Lord. You can see where I'm prone to skirting the issues I need to deal with, and you know when I'm indulging in foolishness when I could be having a meaningful interaction with someone who walks in the truth. I know it's okay to have fun, but it's good for me to look in the mirror regularly as well. Grant me the grace to soak in the wisdom that will change me for the better.

# Evening

The day has been long, Lord, but that's water under the bridge. Bless me now with stillness and sleep. I sigh and turn over, knowing that night will usher in the day with new joys and possibilities, gifts from your ever-wakeful spirit.

# Morning

Lord, I know my friend is overwhelmed right now. Just as you lift my burdens when I come to you in prayer, show me what I can do to make her load lighter. I lay her troubles before you, Lord. I know our efforts can lift her burdens.

# Evening

As for me, I will behold thy face in righteousness: I shall be satisfied, when I awake, with thy likeness.

—Psalm 17:15

# Morning

Alleluia, Lord! How we praise you with our words, our songs, and our lives! When we look back over all the situations you've brought us through, we are so grateful. We are filled with confidence that we can face the future because you will be there with us. And so we just want to stop today and praise you for all you are and all you do! Alleluia and Amen!

# *Evening*

Lord, thank you for being a part of my work today. I can always tell when a thought or an idea comes from you because it's just too perfect to have been my own! That you care enough to be involved in my work is a precious gift to me, Lord—one I would never want to be without.

# Morning

We are blessed by your enveloping spirit as near to us as daily changing weather. Your comfort touches us like gentle rain and hushed snow. And, like the sound of thunder and glimpse of searing lightning, you startle us with new opportunities.

# Evening

Whenever I think of how you cherish me, I am amazed, Father. It's good for me to stop and remember that you actually delight in me, that you gave your most precious sacrifice to save me, and that there is nothing you would withhold from me that would benefit my life. I want to simply rest in the shade of your protective love right now as you impress your love on my heart.

# Morning

Lord, we should not just turn to you in times of trouble, we should run to you. Where else can we find both shelter and consolation? Where else can we feel both completely safe and unconditionally loved? Thank you for opening your arms to us whenever we need to run into them. Help us learn to run to you at the first sign of trouble. You are an unfailing refuge.

# Evening

Lord, when there seems to be no easy way out of a tough situation, I turn to you. When relationships seem too difficult to navigate, I turn to you. When I fear for my safety or feel threatened by bodily harm, I turn to you. You, O Lord, are my sanctuary. With you I am always safe. I praise you for this night and day!

# Morning

Then said Jesus unto the twelve, Will ye also go away? Then Simon Peter answered him, Lord, to whom shall we go? thou hast the words of eternal life. And we believe and are sure that thou art that Christ, the Son of the living God.

—John 6:67–69

# *Evening*

O Lord, some days it seems that every hour is spent in toil, with little time left over for relaxing with loved ones. Help us keep in mind that our hours of work sow seeds of hope. In time, you will comfort us and restore us to a posture of joy and celebration. Thank you, Lord, for understanding both our need to work hard and our need to enjoy this beautiful life.

# Morning

Everything looks much brighter than it did before. My prayer for strength has been answered. My cries for help have been heard. My pleas for mercy flew directly to your throne. Now I'm ready to help my neighbor, Lord. Let me not delay.

# Evening

Lord, sometimes I wonder what you think of this temple you created. There are some leaks in the roof and a few cracks in the walls. I have not always treated my body as a sacred temple for your Spirit. I've had days where I've felt deflated and I've found refuge in a few too many chocolates or a few too many sips of wine. Yet I know that even when I falter, your beautiful Spirit does not abandon ship! May I focus on that truth, Lord, and strive to be the being you want me to be.

# Morning

Like an itch that won't let up, a buzz of creativity is catching our attention and wanting release. Songs whisper to us, wanting melodies; words and paintings are needing paper; dances, our moving feet. Help us recognize your presence in this nudge to movement.

# Evening

Lord, it is tempting to get entangled in the things of this world. When I get too caught up in the rat race or keeping up with the Joneses, prod me to step back, reflect, and call to mind what is truly important: Making time for conversation with you.

# Morning

Lord, I do believe! And because of my hope of life with you in eternity, there is all the more meaning for life today. There's meaning in my choices, my relationships, my work, my play, my worship. It all matters, it all counts, and I live knowing one day I'll stand in your presence with great joy.

# Evening

He that dwelleth in the secret place of the most High shall abide under the shadow of the Almighty. I will say of the Lord, He is my refuge and my fortress: my God; in him will I trust.

—Psalm 91:1–2

May

# Evening

Who shall ascend into the hill of the Lord? or who shall stand in his holy place? He that hath clean hands, and a pure heart; who hath not lifted up his soul unto vanity, nor sworn deceitfully.

—Psalm 24:3–4

# Morning

Lord, bring me to the place where peace flows like a river, where soft green grasses gently hold the weight of my tired body, where the light of a new sunrise casts warmth.

# Evening

You give your help, O Comforting God, not in proportion to our merit, but based only on our need. For you come not only to those who are "keeping it together," but to those of us who are fragmented and fractured. I need the tenderness of your caress so that I know I am not alone in my awful feelings of weakness.

# Morning

God, I feel happy today, and I have you to thank for that. No matter what is going on outside of me, I am strong and safe and secure inside because you love and care for me. Thank you for loving me when I have been cranky, tired, lazy, and even mean. Thank you for being there when I ignored your presence, God. Your steadfast love is a constant reminder of just how good I have it in life. And that makes me happiest of all!

# Evening

Lord, why is it that when I am the most tired or crave sleep myself, the children's bedtime becomes prolonged and difficult? There is always one last drink of water, one final trip to the bathroom, one more bedtime story, or one more postscript to the prayer. By then, desperation sets in, and my temper becomes short.

God of peace, help me to face bedtime more calmly. Help me to discover strategies for helping my children to wind down and relax. Prevent me from losing my temper, and grant me a soothing manner so the children's last memories of the day are pleasant and loving. Thank you, Lord, for your promise of a safe and peaceful sleep.

# Morning

I will hear what God the Lord will speak: for he will speak peace unto his people, and to his saints: but let them not turn again to folly.

—Psalm 85:8

# Evening

Lord, no matter what we bring of ourselves to give you, even if we include all our hopes and dreams, it's never enough to give in return for all you've given to us. And so we give you our praise. We sing to you and come before you with our meager offerings, praying all the while that you will make something marvelous of them.

# Morning

Lord, please forgive us in our impatient moments and nudge us back onto the right path. We live in a society that knows nothing of delayed gratification; we often get caught up in the expectation that everything we need from you and ask of you will happen immediately. But we know from experience that your timing is always perfect, Lord. We are blessed and privileged to have time for reflection and growth.

# Evening

Like the turkey wishbone, God of wholeness, I am being pulled apart by job, family, home, errands, friends, and my needs. I'm preoccupied with what I am not doing and feel the pull to do it all. Help me choose wisely. Remind me to negotiate on the job and at home for the time I need in both places. Remind me, O God, to negotiate for a leaner lifestyle, for I am part of the pull. In the tugging days ahead, be the hinge that keeps my life's parts synchronized in harmonious movement, not split apart at all.

# Morning

Lord, I deeply desire to abide in you. I desire to have you abiding in me as well, so closely that I can speak to you any time and feel your presence. Destroy the distractions that create distance between us, Lord. Clear out the clutter that keeps me from sensing your best plan for my life. Then when I ask for what I wish, it will be the fulfillment of your desire for me as well.

# Evening

I remember hearing someone say once, "If God seems far away, guess who moved?" It's true, Lord: Sometimes I drift far away from you. I neglect reading your Word, I let my prayer life go by the wayside, and I get all tangled up in my attempts to handle everything on my own. I usually come to a sudden realization of how much I need you, and I am grateful for the epiphany! Even though I'm the one who's moved so far away, you don't hold it against me; you simply call me back.

# Morning

Nevertheless I am continually with thee: thou hast holden me by my right hand. Thou shalt guide me with thy counsel, and afterward receive me to glory.

—Psalm 73:23–24

# *Evening*

Held up to your light, our broken hearts can become prisms that scatter micro-rainbows on the wall. Our pain is useless as it is, redeeming God, just as a prism is a useless chunk of glass until light passes through it. Remind us that the smallest ray of sun in a shower can create a rainbow. Use our tears as the showers and your love as the sun. Looking up, we see the tiniest arches of hope in the lightening sky.

# Morning

Lord, how blessed we are to be able to see you all around us and to sense your presence within us. Even though we can't see you in the same way we might see a friend or a neighbor, we see you in your Word and in all that is good and true in the world around us. Thank you, Lord, for making yourself so available to us.

# Evening

Will tomorrow be less hectic and more inclined toward joy? Will I be less tired? God help me, I'm not waiting to find out. In your creation, joy can be found anytime, but mostly now. Keep reminding me that now is all of life I can hold at any moment. It cannot be banked, invested, hoarded, or saved. It can only be spent.

# Morning

On gossamer wings, the angels move as gentle breezes on a summer morning, quietly reminding us that we are always being watched over, always being loved.

# *Evening*

O Lord, I savor this triumph: I met my goal! Day by day, I reached into my heart and found energy to keep on. Day by day, I reached out and found your hand leading, your inspiration guiding. Stand with me to accept applause for our joint success.

# Morning

Lead me in thy truth, and teach me: for thou art the God of my salvation; on thee do I wait all the day.

—Psalm 25:5

# *Evening*

Heavenly Father, when I was young, I thought
all things hurt or broken could be fixed: knees,
feelings, bicycles, tea sets. Now I've learned that not
everything can be repaired, relived, or cured. As a
mother comforts her child, heal my hurting and grant
me the peace I used to know. This I pray. Amen.

# Morning

Lord, today I pray for your grace and mercy to help me to live unselfishly. Putting others first does not come naturally to me, Lord, but with your help, I will stop and think before I speak or act. I'm not at all confident in my ability to do that without you, but I also know that anything is possible when you are involved. Thank you, Lord.

# Evening

Dear God, waiting for you is the hardest part of life. Not knowing. Not understanding. Not being able to figure things out. And when you don't provide answers right away, I feel as if I'll go crazy. But when I stop a moment and think about it, it makes sense that there will be times when you ask me to just trust you, when you'll challenge my rhetoric about believing in you and teach me to be patient. So here I am. I'll be still and wait for you.

# Morning

This morning I am marveling at the birds at the bird feeder, Lord. Those little creatures are so fascinating! Their plumage, the variety of sizes, shapes, beaks, tails, wings . . . I feel a sense of pure delight at their existence. I can find so many things to be in awe of in this great, wide universe you have made. You have made it all to speak of your majesty—to tell us what you are like. I turn my heart toward heaven today, to worship and give glory to you, Lord.

# Evening

Have mercy upon me, O Lord, for I am in
trouble: mine eye is consumed with grief,
yea, my soul and my belly.

—Psalm 31:9

# Morning

Lord, as I walk in your spirit of strength and love today, may others see what life in you is like. It isn't mere religion or a list of rules and regulations. Rather, it's real life full of adventure, challenge, wonder, joy, and peace—all in the context of relationship with you as I live through the energy you provide. Thank you for the spirit of boldness that enables me to live out my faith without fear.

# *Evening*

O Lord, how I pray for the young people I love
as they head out into the world on their own.
Help them tune in to your presence, Lord, and
make them wise beyond their years. Warn them
of dangers and protect them from the schemes of
others. Teach them to love themselves and others
extravagantly, but wisely as well. They are your
children, Lord, and you love them even more than I
do. I place them in your hands.

# Morning

Lord, how many times have I resolved to spend time first thing each morning in your Word and in prayer—and how many times have I neglected to do so! A day that begins with you, Lord, is sure to be a day blessed by you. Give me an insatiable thirst for time with you, Lord. And thank you for always being available to meet with me.

# Evening

O Lord God, who has given us the night for rest, I
pray that in my sleep my soul may remain awake
to you, steadfastly adhering to your love. As I lay
aside my cares to relax and relieve my mind, may I
not forget your infinite and unresting care for me.
And in this way, let my conscience be at peace, so
that when I rise tomorrow, I am refreshed in body,
mind and soul.

—John Calvin

# Morning

Surrounded by a community of headstones, we remember and mourn, celebrate and play, God of history and future. We place our bouquets on overgrown graves and our picnic lunches on family reunion tables. And we feel grateful for our history written by strangers fallen in battle to insure our freedom-filled lives of safety. Our ancestors' efforts are remembered throughout our lives in strengths, names, and accomplishments that we now pause and honor. Bless our picnics and parties as we join in the parade of those remembering, those remembered.

# Evening

Lord, you know how much time and effort I put into surrounding myself with my favorite things. Sometimes I wonder if it's always worth it. Please help me sort out what's truly valuable and what I can do without. One thing I know is worth pursuing is the wisdom found in your Word. As I read it and your Spirit helps me to comprehend it, I feel rich indeed.

June

# *Evening*

I am here right now, Father, because I do want to walk in your ways. I know the key is staying connected to you because the ways of the world are all around me, always imposing a different set of values and a different worldview. Give me a wise and discerning heart in all things today so I can stay on track.

# Morning

Lord, today I want to give you thanks for all the little children who bring so much joy into the world. I feel that they must spring directly from your love for us. How we treasure the hugs and smiles of these little angels, Lord. They are as special to us as they are to you. Lay your hand upon their heads, Lord. Touch them with your grace, and keep them close to you.

# Evening

How precious also are thy thoughts unto me, O God! how great is the sum of them! If I should count them, they are more in number than the sand: when I awake, I am still with thee.

—Psalm 139:17–18

# Morning

We teeter on the edge of splitting up, Lord; help us use this interval as a wake-up call. You link our two halves and can re-create us whole.

# Evening

I need to believe beyond the present darkness, for it threatens to stop me in my tracks. Steady me, God of infinite resources, as I collect my beliefs like candles to light and move through this dark tunnel of doubt and uncertainty. Inspire me to add new truths as they reveal themselves in my life. Along the way, help my unbelief.

# Morning

Blessed Father, when we think of joy, we often think of things that are new—a new day, a new baby, a new love, a new beginning, the promise of a new home with God in heaven. Rejoicing in these things originates with having joy in you who make all things new. Rather than relying on earthly pleasures to provide happiness, we should rejoice in you and in each new day you bring. Joy is a celebration of the heart that goes beyond circumstances to the very foundation of joy—the knowledge that we are loved by you. Help us rejoice in your teachings. Amen.

# *Evening*

Prayer, O God, is as steadying as a hand on the rudder of a free-floating boat and as reliable as sunrise after night. It keeps me going, connected as I am to you, the source of wind beneath my daily wings.

# Morning

All work can be good, Lord, for you can upgrade the most mundane, difficult, or nerve-wracking job into one that matters. God of all skills and vocations, bless and inspire my work; deliver me from boredom and laziness.

# Evening

For who is God save the Lord? or who is a rock save our God? It is God that girdeth me with strength, and maketh my way perfect.

—Psalm 18:31–32

# Morning

We find ourselves here in the pew because somewhere in our lives, clearly or muffled, we heard you call. Here we are, sleepy and alert, worried and assured, certain and doubtful, to hear your message fit for us all.

# Evening

Reach out to me, a child again, lost, frightened, and alone with few answers for comfort. Stay with me until I fall asleep and be here if I awake scared. Let me be a child tonight, Lord. Tomorrow I'll be big and strong and all grown up, but for now, find me, hold me.

# Morning

In my attempts to "get it right" as I order my life and the lives of those in my family, remind me, O Creator God, to look around and see how you have brought order to our world. Such balance, such harmony, such stability. May I find the faith to trust you like a bird trusts the winds that allow it to soar.

# *Evening*

To those scanning a night sky, you sent a star. To those tending sheep on a silent hill, you sent a voice. What sign, Lord, are you sending me to come, be, and do all you intend? Let me hear, see, and accept it when you do.

# Morning

Lord, how freeing it is to rid our drawers and closets of unneeded clothing and pass it along to someone who can really use it! Thanks for reminding us that since you provide for our needs, we don't need to hold on to any surplus. Keep us mindful that true beauty comes not from the latest fashions but from hearts dedicated to sharing your love with the world.

# Evening

May your eyes look kindly upon this family, Lord, for we need your love and guidance in our lives. This is a family that seeks to do the right things—to work hard for a living, to raise up children who will contribute to society, and to be a blessing in our neighborhood. But we know we need your constant help to do these things. May we be filled with love and happiness—all of us who live in this home: by fulfilling our responsibilities, day in and day out; by being accountable in all our actions; by giving whenever we can, even when it hurts; by nurturing warmth and understanding among us. And by always looking out for the best interests of others. Please grant our requests according to your great goodness.

# Morning

Almighty God, there are so many times when we come before you and simply confess, "We don't understand." Keep us from wasting time trying to make sense of the inscrutable! While we never want to stop mining your Word for gems of knowledge, help us find peace in the truths we can fathom and trust you with everything else.

# Evening

The earth and all the inhabitants thereof are
dissolved: I bear up the pillars of it.

—Psalm 75:3

# Morning

Lord, I want my thoughts to be like your thoughts. I want to discern what you discern and have the insight you have into all that happens in the world. I know that can never really be, Lord, but if I am open to your Spirit at all times, perhaps I can construe your hopes now and then. May my mind never be so cluttered that I fail to receive a message you are trying to share with me, Lord.

# *Evening*

Dear God, I long to feel the peace you bring, the peace that passes all understanding. Fill my entire being with the light of your love, your grace, and your everlasting mercy. Be the soft place that I might fall upon to find the rest and renewal I seek. Amen.

# Morning

Lord, today I pray for all those who have sought all the wrong kinds of protection. It's so easy for us to become obsessed with protecting our marriages, our children, and our well-being to the extent that we are in danger of losing our peace of mind. Remind us all, Lord, that when we are in your hands, we are in the best of hands. You will never fail us. You will never renege on your promises. With you, we stand strong and have great hope.

# Evening

Lord, speak to me through these pages.
Let me hear your gentle words
Come whispering through the ages
And thundering through the world.

Challenge me and change me,
comfort me and calm me.
Completely rearrange me,
Soothe me with a psalm.

Teach me how to please you,
Show me how to live.
Inspire me to praise you
For all the love you give.

# Morning

O God, my days are frantic dashes between have to, ought, and should. There is no listening bone in me. Lead me to a porch step or a swing, a chair or a hillside, where I can be restored by sitting, Lord, simply sitting. With you there to meet me, sitting places become prime places for collecting thoughts, not to mention fragmented lives.

# Evening

Dear Lord, I need renewal in my life.
But tell me what you want me to be, first,
then tell me what you want me to do.
Speak, for I am listening,
Guide, for I am willing to follow.
Be silent, for I am willing to rest in your love.

# Morning

We are halfway to Christmas . . . may we be saved from being overly absorbed in the materialism and commercialization of the season, so that our hearts will be filled with the spirit and hope of Christ. O Lord God, keep us watchful for ways that we might ready the world and ourselves for Your rule. May we be strengthened and directed by the assurance of Your love and Your Holy Spirit, in Jesus' Name. Amen.

—James L. Christensen

# Evening

As the hart panteth after the water brooks, so panteth my soul after thee, O God. My soul thirsteth for God, for the living God: when shall I come and appear before God?

—Psalm 42:1–2

# Morning

Lord, how grateful I am that I once again notice the lovely animals all around me. There was a time in my life when I was so busy, I didn't see them at all, though I know they were always there. Now the birds, the deer—even the raccoons—bring me joy every day as I watch them from my window. Catching precious glimpses of these creatures of yours helps me value every moment of every day.

# Evening

God of the strong and the weak, the brave and the fearful, I come before you to place myself in your loving hands. Take my broken places and make them whole. Heal my wounds that I might be strong for you. Give me patience to accept your timing, And help me to trust in your goodness. In your gracious name, I pray. Amen.

# Morning

Lord, I know that all of your commandments are important. I also know, though, that you once said your greatest commandment, after loving you, is for us to love one another. I think love is so important because so many other good things flow from love. If we love those around us, we will never do anything to hurt them. If you see our loving hearts in action, you can overlook and forgive any number of our more minor failures.

# Evening

Lord, you've given me a great team of helpers,
And I'm exceedingly thankful.
Where would I be without them?
They seem to know my needs before I do,
And they jump to meet them.
I know you've given them those gifts of caring,
Of encouragement, of hospitality and healing,
But they're using those gifts as you intended,
To show your love to others—I mean me.
I am thankful to you and to them.
There's not much I can do to pay them back, Lord.
They'd probably refuse a reward anyway.
So I ask you to shower them with blessings,
Just as they have brought blessing to me.
Give them joy and peace in rich supply,
And let your love continue to flow
To them, within them, and through them.

July

# Evening

God, I couldn't help noticing all the loveliness you placed in the world today! This morning I witnessed a sunrise that made my heart beat faster. Then, later, I watched a father gently help his child across a busy parking lot; his tenderness was much like yours. While inside a department store, I spied an elderly couple sitting on a bench. I could hear the man cracking jokes; their laughter lifted my spirits. Then early this evening, I walked by a woman tending her flower bed; she took great pleasure in her work, and her garden was breathtaking. Later, I talked with a friend who is helping some needy families; her genuine compassion inspired me. Thank you, Lord, for everything that is beautiful and good in the world.

# Morning

Thank you for the bright colors of summer! I look around and see the sun in the sky, the clear moon in the night, the brilliance of the flowers and the trees. Thank you, Lord, for blessing me with color in my life. I know that even the darkest, dreariest days cannot last forever, just as the memory of winter fades during summer's glory.

# Evening

O Lord, how precious water is to us, and how parched and desperate we are when it's in short supply. How grateful we are that in you we have access to the living water that will never run dry! Keep us mindful of that refreshing supply today, Lord. Fill us up, for we are thirsty.

# Morning

Your Word really does cut to the heart of the matter when it comes to what life is about, Lord. It doesn't let me hide behind excuses, pretenses, or lies. It gives me the straight scoop without any meaningless frills. That kind of honesty is hard to find in this world—especially accompanied by the absolute love that fuels it. As you lay open my heart with your truth, help me not to run and hide; help me to trust your love enough to allow you to complete the "surgery" that will bring the health and well-being my soul longs for.

# Evening

Lord, I just want to tell you how much I love you, how grateful I am that you have taken me into your care. Ever since I've entrusted myself to you, you've kept me from becoming entangled in the kinds of things that would bring me to ruin. You fill my heart and mind with peace as I stay close to you. It's a miracle of your grace that I am standing tall today, lifting my praise to you from a heart full of love.

# Morning

Bless these tools of my work, Lord. Keep them sharp and strong and ready to do my will. And bless these hands, too, that they might be ready to do all you desire.

# Evening

Let the words of my mouth, and the meditation of my heart, be aceptable in thy sight, O Lord, my strength, and my redeemer.

—Psalm 14:2

# Morning

Lord, we pray for all those in positions of leadership in our government. The pressures and influences on them are of a magnitude we can only imagine. Watch over them, Lord. Reach out to them with your grace, and instill in them your character, your priorities, and your vision for our country and our world.

# Evening

Lord, if I were to boil down all the good news in the universe and look to see what I'd ended up with, there would be the eternal realities of your goodness, your love, and your faithfulness. And in this world, I don't have to look far for them—family, food, shelter, clothing, seasons, tides, sun, moon, stars, life, beauty, truth, salvation. And that's just a sampling, a preview of a much longer list. I'm moved to praise you and to tell you how much I love you back.

# Morning

Thank you, Lord, for the fact that when difficulties and trouble start to accumulate like waters at flood stage, I can find the high ground of safety and security in you. I trust you today—trust your goodness as well as your promises of protection and care for me. And even if everything I own is swept away in the flood, you will still be there with me. Remind me that the stuff of this world is temporary, but my life in you is kept safe both now and for eternity.

# Evening

I have lost some of my zeal to do the work here, God. Forgive me for falling into despair and for being on the lookout for a greener pasture at the expense of full concentration on the tasks at hand. Help me not to cheat my employer by only giving a halfhearted effort.

But most of all, I want to keep my eyes on you, Lord, not on things or places or the myriad circumstances beyond my control. I know that true happiness and fulfillment will come only from being in your will.

And when it is time to move, you will show me. Therefore, strengthen my faith in your goodness. For I know your commitment to me has never been in question. Your zeal for my life never cools. Praise to you!

# Morning

Lord, what comfort I find in the knowledge that you know everything I've ever done. I know going over my sins with you is still necessary for my growth and development, but it helps to know I'll never have to hear you say, "I can't believe you did that!" You know my strengths and my weaknesses. You know my joy and my shame. And yet you still forgive me and have hope for me. Thank you, Lord, for caring enough to truly know me—and for loving me anyway.

# Evening

Creation shouts to me, Lord, about how amazing you are. I see the wonder of your wisdom in everything from the solar system to how bodies of water feed into one another to the life cycles of all living creatures. Everywhere I turn there is something that makes me think about how creative and insightful you are. Thank you for this universe that speaks without words. I hear it loud and clear, and it tells me of your magnificence.

# Morning

Lord, fear has reared its ugly head again and is trying to take me far away from you. Hold me close, Lord. Even though I have momentarily lost my footing in this world, please do not let fear steal the peace I find in you. Give me the strength to turn away from fear and stand tall in the knowledge that I am never alone.

# Evening

Lord, I admit that my light often shines more brightly outside the walls of my home than inside. The truth is that my family members—the ones dearest to me in the world—are usually the first ones to hear my murmuring and arguing and to see my "blemishes." And to add insult to injury, they're often the last ones to hear my confessions and apologies. There are plenty of excuses I could make about being around them more, having to deal with their "blemishes," and about needing to "be me" at home. I want to be consistent in my walk with you, though. Give me the fortitude to shine my light first at home and then into the world around me.

# *Morning*

God, there are so many times throughout my day when my words don't match my actions. I know others are looking to me to be an example of living rightly, but sometimes I just need help keeping my integrity. Help me to not break promises, to watch what I commit to—or overcommit to—especially if I know in my heart I cannot come through. Most of all, match my outer actions to my inner thoughts so that I am walking the talk. I get frustrated when others don't come through with their promises, and I ask that you help me to not become one of those people myself.

# Evening

My heart is fixed, O God, my heart is fixed: I will sing and give praise. Awake up, my glory; awake, psaltery and harp: I myself will awake early.

—Psalm 57:7–8

# Morning

When you say something, Lord God, it is as good as done. It may not take place in the time that I'd imagine or wish, but you are true to your word without fail. So when you tell me not to be anxious—but rather to pray and you will give me your peace—I'll just do that. When you say that you forgive me when I confess my sin, I'll believe that. When you tell me that I'm your child and that you rejoice over me, I'll take pleasure in that. Whatever you say, I'll not doubt it. Thank you for your great and precious promises and for your absolute trustworthiness.

# Evening

Lord, how grateful I am for the gift of hospitality.
When others make me feel welcome in their home,
it fills me with warmth and love. Help me to
cultivate this gift in myself, Lord, so that those who
enter my home may find sweet joy and hope.

# Morning

O Lord, I know you take notice of them—the caretakers for the aged and the ill. They work selflessly for the most vulnerable among us, yet their efforts are so often overlooked. May they sense your presence beside them, Lord. May they feel your strength lifting them up and helping them through the most trying moments. Give them encouragement by helping them see what a difference they make in their patients' lives.

# Evening

Lord, a vexing situation has me very confused. Is it possible I'm trying to sort it out through my own limited understanding and overlooking a crucial element? I know I can trust you with anything. I give this up to you and ask you to restore me to a place where I can look at what's going on in the right way—your way.

# Morning

Lord, what compassion you showered on your people when you grouped us into families! Thank you, Lord, for the homes we are privileged to enjoy. We are thankful for these sanctuaries for our children and grandchildren. May our homes and our families honor you, Lord, in all we say and do within them. Dwell with us, Lord. You are always welcome.

# Evening

Lord, thank you for always listening to my concerns. So often I begin praying in one direction only to sense you turning my thoughts around until I end up praying for something quite different. Only later do I realize you were gently guiding me in a better direction. What blessed communication! I am so grateful.

# Morning

Truth is a narrow road, and it's easy to fall to one side or the other. For every beautiful kernel of truth, there are a thousand lies that can be made around it. Staying on the straight-and-narrow would be impossible if it weren't for God, who leads us to all truth. Delving into God's Word with the Holy Spirit to guide us is the best way to stay on track and keep walking in the truth.

# Evening

Lord, you know all things—from beginning to end—for you are the eternal, all-knowing God. I don't need to fear what is yet to come because I belong to you, and you have given me the gift of eternal life. I come to you today to be refreshed by your presence and your Word.

# Morning

The idea of an exam can strike fear into even the most prepared individuals. But the exam to which God's Word calls us is different from any dreaded math final or set of philosophical questions. This test is a self-checkup to see how we're doing—a chance to ask ourselves some probing questions and to answer them honestly. In the process, if we give ourselves some not-so-good marks, we don't need to beat ourselves up or become discouraged. Instead, we can use what we learn to initiate a fresh starting point for getting back into fellowship with our Lord.

# *Evening*

Well, Lord, since you're offering, I'm not going to be shy about asking. I need wisdom. I need it today as I'm dealing with people and situations and wondering what the best approach or decision might be. Thank you for being generous with your gifts rather than giving them to only a select few. In fact, you make receiving them as simple as just asking. You never cease to amaze me with your generosity, Lord. I'm deeply grateful.

# Morning

Thy word is a lamp unto my feet, and a light unto my path

—Psalm 119:105

# $\mathcal{E}$vening

Lord, please keep me from falling into the trap
of placing any other human on a pedestal. Even
the most spiritual-seeming religious leaders are
riddled with imperfection; they struggle with
sin, just as I do. You alone are perfect and pure,
and you alone are worthy of my adoration. I
promise I will not follow anyone else, no matter
how spiritually enlightened they may seem.
There is no one like you, and you are the only
one who will ever have my full devotion.

# Morning

Lord, so often I believe I know exactly what I think and why, but then I sense your gentle nudging to look at the situation from your perspective. How generous of you to shine your wisdom into the dark corners of my heart and mind! Make me a believer wise in your ways—not one determined to have things my own way.

# Evening

How restful it is to live in your love, Lord God! In the middle of chaos or turmoil, I remember that you are with me, and I am at peace once again. When it seems as if everything is falling apart, you hold me close in your love, and I am able to sleep at night. There is no other source of peace like belonging to you, Father.

# Morning

Lord, sometimes I worry about my loved ones. Though I often complain of the monotony of my day-to-day life, I know my days are full of moments to be treasured. When I hear shocking, horrific stories on the news, I often wonder how I would handle such events if they were to befall me or a loved one. Father, I cling to your promise that you give each of us a future filled with hope. I am grateful that you hear me when I come to you in prayer. Please stay close to me and my loved ones. Grant us the strength to prevail in all circumstances.

# Evening

Over and over I ask myself, O Loving Shepherd, "What can I do?" What can I do to help, to make a difference, to relieve those I love of their hurts? The hardest thing about this mothering role is having others think I can "fix it" and then finding out that I can't, as much as I would like to. Remind me that what you promise is not to "fix it" for us but rather to give us whatever it takes to prevail in spite of our hurts. Help me to see that sharing a tear is sometimes all that is necessary.

# Morning

Dear God, isn't it funny how much better I feel when I choose to love? And yet how many times in the course of my life have I chosen anger or hatred or fear? Let me always choose love first, for when I do make that choice, it opens up the doorway to new friendships and joy that other choices cannot give me. Make love be not only my first choice but my only choice. Thank you, God, for choosing to love me.

# Evening

Ask, and it shall be given you; seek, and ye shall find; knock, and it shall be opened unto you: For every one that asketh receiveth; and he that seeketh findeth; and to him that knocketh it shall be opened.

—Matthew 7:7–8

# Morning

Faith and fear cannot coexist. One always gives way to the other. It is necessary for us to be constantly building up our faith to overcome the numerous sources of destructive disbelief all around us. We need to be continually working at rekindling the gift of God that is in us, which is our faith in him and in his promises. We must be dedicated to developing a spirit of love and power and discipline within ourselves. Studying the words of the scriptures, meditating on them, keeping God's commandments, and praying daily are some of the ways we can keep our faith strong. By focusing on these things, we shut out fear and cultivate faith.

# Evening

The past, O God of yesterdays, todays, and promise-filled tomorrows, can be an anchor or a launching pad. It's sometimes so easy to look back on the pain and hurt and believe the future may be an instant replay. Help us to accept the aches of the past and put them in perspective so we can also see the many ways you supported and nurtured us. Then, believing in your promise of regeneration, launch us into the future free and excited to live in joy.

# Morning

Lord, the only blessing I ask for these days
is to restore my body to good health. When I
am healthy and strong, everything else seems
easier and I have the fortitude to handle
challenges that come my way. Bless me with
good health and vitality, and help me treat my
body right and avoid stress when I can.

# Evening

God, how often do we feel rejection of some sort? I know the sting of not being loved by someone I was once in love with, or the denial of a dream job, or just feeling as though I cannot do anything right. But you never judge, you never deny, you never reject me. May I also offer my own love without judgment and rejection, and give of it freely to anyone who might be lifted up or healed in some small way by my gesture of kindness and compassion.

# Morning

Lord, I open my eyes and all I see are the blessings that surround me. In this moment, I want for nothing, and I live with the knowledge that I can always turn to you for help, and cast my cares upon you, when my clarity and my vision cloud with worry. Thank you, Lord, for reminding me that the joyful blessings of this moment are all because of your love for me.

# Evening

Lord, it's hard to count your blessings when all around you is chaos and despair. Though my heart is heavy and my mind cluttered, please help me to realize that before a flower can show its beauty to the sun, it first is a seed buried in the dirt. Help me to stand above the negative things in life and cast my eyes instead upon the positives that are always there, like the seedling, growing toward the moment when it will appear above ground, face to the sun.

# Morning

Surely I have behaved and quieted myself, as a child that is weaned of his mother: my soul is even as a weaned child.

—Psalm 131:2

# Evening

Lord, I never imagined when I was young that growing older could be such a blessing. The experience and the wisdom I have now about how life works—these are gifts I would never trade for anything. Some people dread their later years, but mine are so blessed—I can only imagine how good the rest of my days will be. Thank you, Lord, for allowing me the privilege of getting older.

# Morning

There is an opposition in all things, and there are all kinds of life circumstances that can erode our faith. What are some "flaming arrows" that might come in our direction? Doubt and fear, sadness and depression? Temptations, both to the body and the spirit? What about financial and employment problems, marriage problems, and health problems? All these and more might be the "flaming arrows" spoken of in the Bible. But we must remember we have faith as our shield! A shield is a versatile and effective means of defense in any battle we might face. Our faith can defend us against any onslaught.

# *Evening*

God, how long have I looked outside of myself for the blessings that were waiting all along? How often have I complained to you about life not being the way I wanted it when I already had what I needed to change? I now know that the blessings of prosperity and joy are all an inside job. By turning first to you, dear God, all else is then opened before me. You taught that your Kingdom was within, not without, and yet once we recognized it, we would also see it all around us. Thank you, God.

# Morning

Today I will think about the miracles in my life. I am thankful that God gives me these special gifts. Miracles remind me that God is always in my life. Thank you, Lord, for showing me your power and surprising me with these moments of grace. Help me see your hand at work and trust that your way is the best.

# Evening

Trust in the Lord, and do good; so shalt thou dwell
in the land, and verily thou shalt be fed.

—Psalm 37:3

# Morning

I am so grateful for my home! It may not be fancy, but it is my own place. How lucky I am to have a place to live safely. How good it is sometimes to retreat from the world and be alone with my things, my routines, and my space. Thank you, Lord, for giving me shelter and a place to call my own.

# *Evening*

Lord, I have a lot of people in my life who let me down and make promises they don't keep. My greatest blessing is knowing that you will never go back on your promises to me and that I can always turn to you for anything. You never fail to give me what I need and to withhold from me the things that I might think I need but really don't. Your wisdom guides me in all my ways, and your promise of eternal love is the only true blessing I desire.

# Morning

Dear Lord, I am blessed to have such good friends in my life, friends who share my sadness and my joy, my pain and my excitement, and who are always there for me when I need them. Just as I can lean on you for anything, Lord, I know you have given me these angels on earth who I can lean on as well. The love of these wonderful people fills my soul. I could not imagine living without them. May I always do for them what they have done for me.

# *Evening*

God, a call, a note, and a handclasp from a friend are simple and seemingly insignificant. Yet you inspire these gifts from people we have a special affection for. These cherished acts of friendship nudge aside doubts about who we are when we feel low and encourage our hearts in a way that lifts our spirits. Thank you for the friends you have given us.

# Morning

God, as much as I don't want to, I can't help but listen to your love, which calls me to always seek to make my enemies my friends. How I have grown to truly dislike the call of this love! I would rather love a stranger than an enemy. This is not easy to even want to do! Still, I know that this is what you want me to do in order to make your love real in my life. And so, Lord, flood me with your love because this call is a hard one for me. Amen.

# *Evening*

Hope is an anchor to the soul. It can keep us from drifting aimlessly, getting caught in whirlpools, or running into sandbars. This anchor is essential in a world so full of various waves. Sometimes those waves slap us from behind; sometimes we see them coming but cannot get out of the way. In all cases, hope ties us to safety. The waves come and go in their fury or playfulness—but hope is always there.

# Morning

He shall spare the poor and needy, and
shall save the souls of the needy.

—Psalm 72:13

# Evening

I confess, Lord, that in my haste to come to you
in prayer and to present my daily laundry list of
requests, I forget the other side of prayer. I forget
to listen for your answer. I know that if I am
patient enough, your gentle message will come to
me when I wait for it. Forgive me my impatience,
Father, when I ask for your help with my children,
then fail to listen to your response. Thank you for
teaching me that if I seek, I will find. Help me to
seek and listen for your answers, written across the
pages of my heart.

September

# Evening

How exciting it is to see and hear the busy hum of a city! I am thankful for all the people who live and work in cities. They have created places that thrum with life and energy. Great things can come from that energy, and I am grateful for the experiences cities provide to all of us.

# Morning

Rain patters down, making puddles everywhere. I wasn't expecting the rain, but I am grateful for its beauty. I look up and see the thickness of the gray clouds and think of a soft blanket. I listen to the rain pour down and think of how it waters the earth to bring new life. Thank you, Lord, for the gift of a rainy day.

# Evening

How beautiful is the work of your hands, Lord! I am grateful for the world of nature. How wonderful it is to see the plants and animals you have created. How awesome is your power on the shape of the Earth! Thank you, Lord, for making the landscape and creating so much beauty in the natural world.

# Morning

Thank you, Lord, at the harvest time. Thank you for the plants that grow to give us food and thank you for the people who grow them. The earth's bounty is a miracle! As I enjoy fresh food, may I always be grateful for what I eat and the nutrition it provides.

# *Evening*

But as for me, my prayer is unto thee, O Lord, in an acceptable time: O God, in the multitude of thy mercy hear me, in the truth of thy salvation. Deliver me out of the mire, and let me not sink: let me be delivered from them that hate me, and out of the deep waters.

—Psalm 69:13–14

# Morning

I'm getting a crick in my neck trying to see around the bend, God of past and future. I'm wearing myself out second guessing. Teach me to live in today, needing just a small glimpse down the road. No need to borrow trouble that may not be waiting.

# Evening

Bless my family, O God, for it is unique . . . some say
too much so. I am grateful you know we are joined
by love—for each other and for and from you. We are
grateful you use more than one pattern to create a good
family. This pioneering family has you at its heart.

# Morning

Let me do what lies clearly at hand, this very minute. Grant me the insight to see that too much planning for the future removes me from the present moment. And this is the only existence, the only calling I have been given—right now to do what is necessary. Nothing more, nothing less. Thus may I use this next moment wisely.

# Evening

O God, you have called each of us to special tasks, purposes, and vocations, equipping us with the skills and energy to perform them. For some, our vocations send us into the labor force; for some, it is soon bringing retirement. For some, it is in full-time homemaking. For some, our vocations are in artistic skills; for some, in volunteering, helping, neighboring. Always, there is that first call from you, God of vision, working through our work to help, heal, change a needful world.

# Morning

Strengthen our resolve, O God, to take better care of ourselves, for we eat, drink, and choose risky lifestyles and then want to blame you! As we live with our consequences, help us know you as the loving parent who weeps first when your children get themselves into trouble.

# Evening

You love us Lord, not because we are particularly lovable. And it's certainly not the case that you need to receive our love. I am so heartened by this: You offer your love simply because you delight to do it.

# Morning

When I freeze in worry and indecision, fill me with the trusting contentment of a child swinging on a garden gate in arcs of slow, free motion. Your presence is oil for the hinges.

# *Evening*

I will bless the Lord, who hath given me counsel:
my reins also instruct me in the night seasons. I
have set the Lord always before me: because he is
at my right hand, I shall not be moved.

—Psalm 16:7–8

# Morning

Today I need your help, God, feeling the need for a breath of fresh air. The old habits and attitudes I've clung to for so long seem stale and worn out. Renew me from the inside out, starting now!

# *Evening*

We come, needing your help to move beyond: the times we hurt one another and the times we willingly misunderstand, cherishing our differences and the times we assume we know all there is to know about each other and turn away. And then there are the times that we make private rules only to publicly condemn anyone who fails to abide by them, limiting one another by labeling, interpreting, conditioning, insisting, resisting, defining. From all this, Lord, we come, asking that you forgive us as we forgive those "others" we need new eyes to see and ears to hear. Be with us as we do so.

# Morning

Okay, Lord, I know "it's only stuff," but much of it is useful, and I want to take good care of it. Help me see the line between wanting to be a good steward and caring too much about material things. That line is often blurry from my earthly perspective. Help me be a responsible caretaker without putting too much value on mere "stuff."

# Evening

Thank you, Lord, for reddened eyes. Believing your promise that comfort follows mourning, we bawl and sob. In your wisdom, onion-peeling salty tears differ from cleansing grieving ones; we're grateful for their healing. Deliver us from stiff upper lips, and if we've lost our tears, help us find them.

# Morning

Enliven my imagination, God of new life, so that I can see through today's troubles to coming newness. Surround me with your caring so that I can live as if the new has already begun.

# Evening

Tossing leaves onto a fire, we name them as regrets and failures from which we choose to be free. We trust you to redeem even these, our deadest moments. They, like autumn leaves, can make the brightest blaze. Stir new possibilities into life from the embers; fan the sparks of dreams so that we may become one with your purpose for us. It is the root from which we, leaf and human life, begin and from which the most amazing new creation can burst into being, a flame in the darkness.

# Morning

I want to pray for the children in my life, Father. They're so innocent, and this world can sometimes be a harsh place. Thank you for assigning them a special place in your care and for giving their guardian angels direct access to you at all times. Be with them today, protect them—heart, soul, mind, and body. I know they will thrive in your love.

# Evening

May I be blessed in this suffering. May I know that you can use this thing to show me a mistaken attitude, a destructive behavior. In that way, may I be blessed in this suffering, O Lord, my God.

# Morning

Lord, today I ask your special blessing on the elderly among us. No matter how old we are, we notice our bodies aging. How difficult it must be to be near the end of life and struggling to hold on to mobility, vision, hearing, and wellness of being. Give us compassion for those older than we are, Lord, and thank you for your promise that you will be with us to the very end of our days.

# *Evening*

It is vain for you to rise up early, to sit up late, to eat the bread of sorrows: for so he giveth his beloved sleep.

—Psalm 127:2

# Morning

Thank you for your wise ways, Lord. Following them fills my life with true blessings—the riches of love and relationship, joy and provision, peace and protection. I remember reading in your Word that whenever I ask for your wisdom from a faith-filled heart, you will give it, no holds barred. So I'll ask once again today for your insight and understanding as I build, using your blueprints.

# Evening

Life is full of trade-offs, Lord, and I need to make one. I want to venture off the fast track where I'm losing more than I'm gaining. Guide my search for a job where I can have both a life and a living. Restore my balance, not the checkbook kind, for it will change when I do. Your balance is not found running in a circle, but along a beckoning path where enough is more than sufficient; where money comes second to family, community, and self; where success takes on new meaning; and where, in the giving up, I gain wealth beyond belief.

# Morning

Stumbling happens. Don't I know it! I can get bummed out just by reviewing my mistakes and mess-ups from yesterday. But thankfully, I don't need to! God has hold of my hand. My worst blunders—even if they've been truly harmful to myself or others—are not the end of the world. God will bring a new day, a fresh start, a redeemed relationship, a restored soul.

# Evening

Lord, only you can comfort us when we grieve. The heaviness we feel at such times can make even breathing a struggle. But you, O Lord, stay close. You fill us with your peace and your comfort. You never let us retreat completely from your light into the darkness of despair. And finally, in your time, you restore joy to our souls. We are ever so grateful, O Great Comforter.

October

# *Evening*

Lord, I knew the minute the words were out of my mouth that they would have been better left unsaid. Why do I continue to fall into the trap of needing to say what I think at the expense of someone else? Not only did I hurt someone's feelings, but I also looked like a fool in the process! Help me to repair the damage and learn from this experience. Give me another chance to behave nobly by saying nothing.

# Morning

Lord, how I love to wake up to a cool, crisp fall day with snowcapped mountains in the distance and the blue sky above. On mornings like this I think, What a wonderful day to be alive! I soon realize, however, that I should see each day of my life as an extraordinary gift. Help me to remember to value each day, Lord. And may I find in each of them a way to bring glory to you.

# *Evening*

Everything around me keeps changing, Lord. Nothing lasts. My relationships with others are different than they were before. I started to feel as if there is nothing sure and steady on which I can depend. Then I remembered your ever-present, unchanging love. Through these transitions, your love gives me courage and hope for the future. Amen.

# Morning

Lord, even though I know worry is a useless waste of time and energy, it snares me again and again. Thank you for helping me notice early on that I'm about to wallow in worry once more. As I give this situation to you, Lord, I release my need to worry about it as well. Instead, I look for the blessings in the midst of all that's going on and thank you wholeheartedly for them. I willingly trade my worry for your peace.

# *Evening*

O satisfy us early with thy mercy; that we
may rejoice and be glad all our days.

—Psalm 90:14

# Morning

Today I take joy in nature. I look around and see all that you have made. The natural world is full of your presence. Thank you for the birds migrating overhead, for the wind's breath, even for the violence of a thunderstorm. I know that everything came to be by your hand, and the world around me is a blessing in my life.

# *Evening*

Listen to the wind! I am thankful for its power.
The wind is a gift that freshens the air and scrubs it
clean. Without the wind, our weather would never
change. Thank you, God, for the blessing of the
wind and the power it has to change our world and
make all things fresh and new.

# Morning

Lord, I know I encounter them every day: your loved ones who are—on their own strength—desperately trying to make some sense out of this life. Help me reach out to them. Give me the words to say and the gentle approach that will lead them to the knowledge of you and to the immense blessings you want to bestow on them.

# Evening

Some people feel guilty for resorting to prayers of desperation. But God never turns away anyone who sincerely turns to him for help. Even when we've been distant, not walking close to him, he doesn't despise our cries for help as we look to get in step with him again.

# Morning

Help me, Lord, when I wake up with a belly full of fearful butterflies. My fears of earthly concerns are a dark distraction, but my awe of you and your works is what will help me power through the day.

# Evening

Each time in our lives has strengths and liabilities, the same way time passes and good and bad things happen to the whole world. But we can't spend too much time focusing on every individual thing that happens, like a blip in the stock ticker. We must live each day in God's love while we live our whole lives in God's hands.

# Morning

Help me rise in the morning like a thriving hardy plant in bloom, Lord, growing in the nurturing soil of my life of faith and works. With a sturdy foundation in your promises and holy word, I can grow tall in the light of your love.

# $\mathcal{E}$vening

Lord, what's so enchanting about a false prophet? Reflecting back on the charmers and even charlatans I've known makes me feel ashamed of my poor judgment, but I take heart that those times are few out of my life. Having one true prophet in my life takes the wind out of any charlatan's sails.

# Morning

Lord, I know I need a vacation when the first thing on my to-do list is finding yesterday's to-do list. But there's no time to pause my life and step back to recharge, at least not for more than a minute. Help me to center myself in your love, take a deep breath, and dive back in.

# *Evening*

Guide my footsteps, Lord,
To that blessed place
Where pain and sorrow are washed away
Under the sunshine of your love.

# Morning

There are two kinds of pride. One is self-respect. The other is conceit: an exaggerated view of your own abilities. It's a cliche that parents or teachers say "Because I said so!" as the last line of reasoning against obstinate kids, but more of us think something like this than we probably want to admit. The only one who ever really just "said so" is God. Try to remember this when something frustrating seems out of your control.

# *Evening*

Being optimistic and upbuilding with others is a daily choice that is decided with both the mind and the heart. I know God loves me and I have faith, but bad news, confrontations, and even rude drivers add up to a lot of negativity every day. I need to think bigger than these earthly worries—tragedy and loss are very real, but what God has in store for all of us is so big we can't even imagine it.

# Morning

Hope is knowing that no matter how bad "all this" seems, God is still all good. Today and every day, God is good. Tomorrow and forever, God is good.

# Evening

Lord, help me calm my mind amid the tumult of a busy week. Faith is a silent declaration of inner wholeness amidst the outer appearance of chaos and disorder. Everything might be swirling around in our home and outside it, but I know my family and my faith in you are rock solid.

# Morning

Lord, today I want to help someone. Every day—or, honestly, most days—I pray for guidance or to say thank you. But sometimes I forget that part of loving you and living in your light is to be a conduit for that love and light. We are most like angels when we stand ready to channel the good inside of us.

# *Evening*

Poised on the brink of new beginnings, I've discovered that I either find a ladder to climb or learn to fly. Turning to God with my trust and faith is the best way to find the path forward.

# Morning

Lord, lately I really do feel like a tree that has been chopped down. Hope seems far away. I have not forgotten, though, that you are a God of new life. I trust that the sun will shine again and the rain will fall when necessary. I will not allow myself to remain so shaken. I will hold steadfast to hope.

# *Evening*

Competition can be a wonderful resource if it results in dreams fulfilled rather than rivalry suffered. God made us and extended grace to us so we could live meaningful lives and walk through the world doing good (2 Corinthians 9:8). Turn away from a rivalry and toward God. When you look again, you may have a new ally and supporter.

# Morning

Good friends are like clean windows—they let in the light and keep out the rain. Thank you, Lord, for the people you've sent to help me solve crises and celebrate victories in equal measure.

# Evening

Remember your favorite teachers? Teachers need to have a love of learning, an inquisitive mind, and a sense of humor. Jesus is the son of God but also, in daily life, a teacher of extraordinary things. His proverbial door was always open to those who wished to learn, and he wanted to talk with people from all walks of life so he could continue to learn as well.

# Morning

If God has a plan for us all, am I ever in control?
Through the eyes of faith, I see the work of angels
daily orchestrating my life on behalf of our heavenly
conductor. Like a train, I can choose where to get on
and where to get off. If I don't like where I've chosen
to go, I can put my faith in God, get back on the train,
and see where the next stop is.

# *Evening*

I cannot wander so far in any direction, vigilant God, that you are not already there. When my days are relatively predictable, it's easier to make sure I take time to find you in my thoughts. Help me remember you when life takes me to new places where I feel stressed or depressed.

# Morning

Angels find us not only when we need them most, but when we simply need them. Don't wait until you face a catastrophe to change gears from daily prayers of gratitude to questions or requests. God challenges us sometimes but also wants to make our lives easier overall, both through faith and because being tested makes us stronger.

# *Evening*

Hold on to your dreams; they will help guide you on your own path to happiness. Asking God for help in a consistent way and thanking him for the blessings you receive is a great way to stay mindful and grateful. You'll remind yourself every day what you're working for and who's on your side.

# Morning

Sometimes it is so hard to take chances! Thank you, God, for giving me the courage to take a chance and try something new. I am so glad to be able to step out of my comfort zone and find the courage to change. What a gift to know that taking a chance could change my life! Thank you for the excitement of being brave.

# *Evening*

Amidst hobgoblins and pranksters, O God, we seek a quiet corner this autumn evening to give thanks for the saints whose day this really is. Be tolerant of our commercialized, costumed hoopla, even as you remind us of the pillars upon which our faith rests today. Keep our trick-or-treating fun, clean, and safe and our faith memories aware, for it is too easy to lose track of what we really celebrate in the darkness of this night.

November

# Evening

Heavenly Father, we are thankful for family. Please bring our family together in happiness. Help us see everything as your children do: with wonder and awe. Glorious are your creations! Thank you for creating us. We love our family. We love you. Amen.

# Morning

Taking part in family traditions is such a joyous experience! Today I will take time to recall the traditions I experienced as a child and the family times I shared with those around me. I am grateful for those memories and for the opportunity to share those traditions with my family and friends today. Continuing a tradition feels like taking joyful steps along a path from the past to the future.

# Evening

Lord, how important it is for us to be thankful at all times. It's so easy to fall into the trap of having specific expectations and then despairing when events take an unexpected turn. You are working in our lives every moment, Lord. We will do our part by working hard and taking full advantage of all opportunities that come our way, but we also know that some matters are reserved for you. We are thankful that nothing is beyond your control, Lord, and we are grateful that you are our wise leader.

# Morning

As we face worrisome days, restore our funny bones, Lord. Humor helps rebuild and heal, sparking hope and igniting energy with which to combat stress, ease grief, and provide direction.

# Evening

Families are circles of love in which no one wants to be the first to let go of someone else's hand. But as my kids get older and more independent, each fall brings more and more chances for them to let go of my hand. Friends and relatives get busier with their own families and the march toward winter can feel pretty lonely. Lord, help me see what's there all the time: the people who love me, even when they have their own lives.

# Morning

Lord, after a hard day and at the beginning of a new one, I feel depleted and sometimes hopeless. Help me remember that you chose to make me as part of the whole world. Created beings, we are all made, angels and babies and planets alike. We are created, loved, and filled with the wonder of discovery.

# Evening

Birds begin singing again before the storm has fully ended, having known all along that clouds cover—not banish—the sun. Even the night after a storm feels clearer and calmer, like the darkness is a soothing friend rather than a frightening impediment.

# Morning

For God so loves us, his children, that he sent a heavenly host of angels to guide, protect, and inspire us. We may wake up and prepare ourselves for challenges, make plans and backup plans, and synchronize our watches. But even if everything else fails, God is on our side and his host of protectors are there for us.

# Evening

Lord, I've made a small fool of myself again. I pray for the strength to fess up, but admitting a mistake is just the first small step. Learning from it requires a great leap. Please help me to shore up my courage and do the right thing.

# Morning

I don't know what the future holds, but I know who holds the future. Today, I want to try hard to give myself over to God's plan. I can work toward my goals and do my best but I also have to understand that it isn't all up to me or my family or my boss— God is in charge and I trust in his plan.

# Evening

Lord, help me make amends to someone I've hurt. I didn't mean to do it, but it's hard to stay mindful when life gets busy and I'm trying to get a million things done. I lost my temper and it's still on my mind. Being sorry is the beginning of being forgiven. Being forgiven is the beginning of being free. Help me find the words to apologize and make it up to my loved one.

# Morning

Every person has a special gift. One may be a computer whiz; another may have the gift of being a gracious host. God has given each person a unique array of talents and vulnerabilities, and his machinations are beyond our understanding. Respect the gifts of others as you wish to be respected for your gifts.

# Evening

Lord, you have told us to remember the days of old. Memorials have played a large part in the history of your people in Israel, and we thank you for these reminders to honor the past.

As we remember those who have gone before us, we teach our children love and respect for life itself. In giving honor to others, we thank and honor you, O God, for your love and for the great sacrifice of your son, Jesus Christ.

# Morning

How blessed the one who can walk this journey with a light grip on everything. For all will be released, sooner or later. And I wish to practice now, Lord— moment by moment—the letting go. Today, help me understand what to catch and what to release.

# *Evening*

To believe in God's love is to celebrate a reality you cannot see, to respect a realm you're not yet ready for.

# Morning

Even the most accomplished seamstress will tear her fabric in order to create a wearable garment. "To every thing there is a season" (Ecclesiastes 3:1), including to tear and to sew. John Donne asked for holy healing from God to break him down and rebuild him as a better and more godly man. A crisis is an opportunity to mend a crack and make the join even stronger.

# Evening

Lord, today I felt lonely and my imagination ran away with me. Imagine, no hearty knocks at the front door and no welcoming smiles. No supportive hugs and reassuring pats on the back. Without companionship, life would be so sad. But then I remember—God will always be my friend.

# Morning

What transforms ordinary events into lifelong traditions? What makes paper chains into holy relics and gluey, lopsided homemade gifts into icons? Love! Inspire me to show my kids the divine love, the holiness, in the ordinary.

# Evening

The path of love is never easy. Yet it is in the ups and downs, the times of trouble and need, that together you forge a bond strong enough to withstand whatever the road ahead may bring.

# Morning

When you're in too deep, over your head, it's never too late to call for help. Most of us pray the hardest during our worst moments, but that doesn't make our prayers any more heartfelt. In fact, reaching for God's love when you feel overwhelmed can help you remember how God is there for you no matter what, and help you renew that connection when you're feeling better, too.

# *Evening*

Like children pouring ocean water into a hole in the sand, O God, we love you to the best of our ability but can't fathom the size of your love in return.

# Morning

It is empowering to know that I can choose to be happy and whole each moment of each day. Though outside events may change, I remain strong, steadfast, and unwavering when I remember that the choice is mine. Lord, help me understand that the challenges I am going through serve to empower me.

# Evening

We are often harsh because we are afraid—afraid of being hurt. We can take a lesson from the angels who trust their creator and do not fear; they can touch their charges with a gentle hand. God guides us and we can trust him with our vulnerabilities.

# Morning

Having faith is believing that even small things have significance. People of faith believe that every person matters, even one person can make a difference, and that God takes small things and makes them into great things. Today and every day, take one step and then another. Walk with God and make a difference with even the small things you do.

# Evening

Thank you, God, for taking this little lump of clay and molding me into someone who dares to dream and loves to love others. Your attention gives me form, your word gives me power, and your belief in my purpose shapes my destiny.

# Morning

Love makes us greater
than we ever were before,
takes what we have to give
and gives back even more.

Love makes us stronger
than we ever thought we'd be,
takes the load we have to bear
and sets our spirits free.

# *Evening*

Finally, I've emerged from a dark night—into the light with new energy, renewed vigor, feeling strong and healthy. Thank you for tenacity and wholeness. And bless me as I tell others how good you are!

# Morning

Lord, children ask the most amazing questions. Parents and "grownups" are supposed to have all the answers; help me live with my ignorance. Remind me that I don't need all the answers, just a willingness to consider the questions and honor the questioners. I'll always be childlike in the face of your wisdom.

# Evening

Bless us as we weather a family conflict, Lord. We all have certain needs to be met, certain ways of trying to fulfill our dreams. Yet each of us seeks this one basic thing in the midst of it all: love. Simply love. Help me remind my family that our love is steadfast and our need for love is steadfast too.

# Morning

Longtime friendship is a two-way mirror, O God, a gift from you that returns our best selves reflected in the joy others get from just having us around. Thank you for the gift of perseverance that keeps old friendships new.

# *Evening*

God grant you the joy of learning, as you seek spiritual direction. Listen to those who are wise in the ways of the spirit. Hear the inner workings of your own heart. And grow closer to God.

# Morning

Lord, no matter what our personal battles are this holiday season, we rest assured that you are with us every moment. Family relationships can be strained this time of year. Feelings can be easily trampled. But what better time to focus on all the blessings we have (even if some of them come in the form of difficult relatives!). Deliver us from any ill will, Lord, and keep us focused on all the reasons we have to be thankful.

# Evening

Dear God, your peace is like the sweet calm air after a storm, like a warm blanket on a cold winter day, like a happy smile of someone I love on a day when nothing has gone right. Your peace brings me the comfort and the strength I need to get through the hardest of times and the thickest of situations. I am so grateful, God, for the kind of peace your presence offers me, a peace so deep and abiding I know that no matter what is happening, that peace is there for me to tap into. Like an overflowing well at the center of my being, your presence is the water that quenches my thirst and gives me renewed vigor and life. Thank you, God, for your everlasting peace.

# Morning

Today, in the dreary days as we head toward winter, I celebrate flowers. How wonderful it is to see their bright colors. I am grateful for the chance to bring flowers into my home to brighten a dreary day. Thank you for the colors and smells of spring and the opportunity to welcome them into my life at any time of year.

# *Evening*

Jesus was the fulfillment of God's promise of salvation. His life and death made salvation possible for us. What a glorious, selfless gift! I ponder this blessing every day, and gratitude and joy fill my very being.

December

# *Evening*

Out of the south cometh the
whirlwind: and cold out of the north.

—Job 37:9

# Morning

Father, instill in me the gifts of humor and joy. Teach me how to lift downcast spirits and dispense the medicine of good cheer in your name.

# *Evening*

We're caught up in well-worn, comfy traditions, Lord. Keep them worthy, for like a deer path through the forest, they lead us forward and back. Thank you for the divine love and holiness found in the ordinary.

# Morning

My Creator, blessed is your presence. For you and you alone give me power to walk through dark valleys into the light again. You and you alone give me hope when there seems no end to my suffering. You and you alone give me peace when the noise of my life overwhelms me. I ask that you give this same power, hope, and peace to all who know discouragement, that they, too, may be emboldened and renewed by your everlasting love.

# Evening

God of my heart, I am a broken person. I do not know how to handle this suffering. I am not strong enough to do it alone. Be my strength, God, and do for me what I simply cannot do for myself. Be the glue that binds the pieces of my shattered soul back together, that I may rise and step back onto the joyful path of life again. Amen.

# Morning

"Incomplete" is stamped all over my life, Lord, for I can't get everything done. Help me learn to separate what can be finished from what can't, giving today only today's measure of tasks.

# *Evening*

Lord, it gets so crowded when everyone's home for the holidays—and there can be strife! It's easy for us to long for a quick return to our quieter day-to-day lives. Don't let our desire for peace and quiet rob us of the joy of spending time with loved ones, Lord! You've blessed us with quiet times and celebratory times, and we want to make the most of both.

# Morning

Lord, so often I keep doing the same things over and over and getting the same unsatisfying results. This is when I need for you to shine your light on my life and reveal to me all that I haven't been able to see through human eyes. You have all knowledge and every answer to the mysteries of heaven and earth. Show me, Lord. Give me just a bit more of the knowledge you possess. Thank you.

# Evening

O Lord, how magnificent is your work on this earth. We can stand at the seashore and feel our own souls rising and filling with your majesty as we marvel at the tides. Or we can walk down a trail and notice that each and every twig has been frosted individually with more icy flakes than we can imagine. We praise you for this awesome creation you share with us, Lord. The more we see of it, the more amazed we are. To you be the glory!

# Morning

Lord, this morning as I was folding a beautiful quilt a
friend made for me, I thought again about how all the
parts of our lives come together to form something
beautiful and useful. Even the mistakes I would love to be
able to erase from my memory helped make me who I am
today; I'm grateful I've been able to see the good that could
come of them. May I always look back without regret and
look forward with hope, knowing that when all is said and
done my life will have been full—and wonderful.

# Evening

Tangled in tape, lists, and holiday wrappings, we are all thumbs of excitement! Bless the surprises we've selected, wrapped, and hidden. Restore us to the joy of anticipation. We want to be surprised, too. Our wish lists include the gift of peace possibilities, of ears to hear a summons and eyes to spot another's need or triumph, of being able to make a difference. As we cut and tape, God of surprises, remind us to keep in touch with the gift's recipient after the wrapping papers are long gone and the ornaments packed.

# Morning

Give me the tools for building peace, O God, when tempers flare—inside and outside these four walls. In your wisdom I daily try to impart, needed tools include a kind heart and faith that measures each tiny rebuilt bridge a triumph.

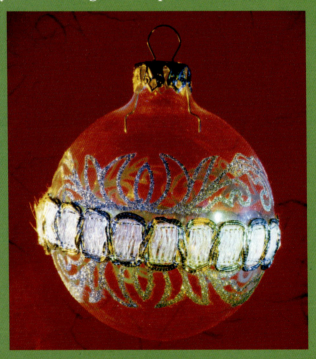

# Evening

When the nights seem long, the days feel like a struggle, and the spirit is weary, we find a resting place in God's enduring love, and we know that his plan for us is good. This is the true meaning of letting go and letting God's higher will be done in our lives.

# Morning

Angels give, love, and teach because they exist to help us be more giving and more loving and more wise. When we suffer, angels wrap their wings around us to comfort and protect us and give us time to heal. When we are stronger, angels unfold their wings and set us free, ready to experience life again. We do well to receive their gifts and watch for their lessons and listen for their messages.

# *Evening*

Lord, help me stay compassionate during stressful family times. Compassion is the ability to walk in another's shoes, even if they are several sizes too small. Compassion is understanding another's challenges, even if they are not our own. Compassion is caring for the welfare of others, even if they are different from us—especially then.

# Morning

Light as a feather and quieter than snow, God flits and flurries through your life, engaged in all your concerns. And like a fresh blanket of snow, God's love quiets the world and gives everyone a fresh start on a bright winter's day.

# Evening

Dear God, show us ways we can help your hurting, needful world. Our children need to see we are not helpless or hopeless but that all efforts, small as they might seem, can matter. Your world could use our creative kind of parenting.

# Morning

Sometimes in the hazy morning between "waking up" and "not yet," take the time to listen to your own soul. You'll find you can hear your angels telling you to be ready for the day. It's the best wake-up call there is.

# *Evening*

Thank you, Lord, for the love you never fail to offer, the help you never fail to give, and the peace I feel when I spend time in your word and the light of your love. Without you, my life would be half empty. With you, I feel happy, whole, and complete.

# Morning

Please give me the tools for building peace, O God, when tempers flare—inside and outside these four walls. In your wisdom I daily try to impart, the tools we need include a kind of heart and faith that considers each tiny rebuilt bridge to be a triumph. The holidays are stressful but they're ultimately about love, faith, and togetherness.

# Evening

We can relax, O Lord, on this the longest darkness of the year, knowing that in order for trees to blossom and bear fruit and the maple tree to yield its sugar, a resting stillness of dormancy is a welcome part of growth.

# Morning

Sometimes when the load we carry is just too much we wonder what good are the angels who are supposed to help us carry it. What we don't notice is that they are often right beside us, telling us it's time to lay it all down.

# *Evening*

Lord, I have decided to be attentive to others's needs rather than try to silence them. This means that I have to take time out of my busy schedule to listen. While I may experience some inconvenience, I expect the rewards of lending an ear to be worthwhile.

# Morning

In the lights and glimmer of modern Christmas decorations we see a tiny speck of brilliance that is the reality angels see, share, and return to when their task on earth is complete. It's a brilliance we can one day see for ourselves when our task is done as well.

# Evening

There's more, much more to Christmas
Than candlelight and cheer;
It's the spirit of sweet friendship
That brightens all the year;
It's thougthfulness and kindness,
It's hope reborn again,
For peace, for understanding
And for good will to men!

# Morning

Lord, how grateful we are that our spirits don't have to sag once the excitement of Christmas is over! For the gift you gave us at Christmas, your beloved son among us, is a gift that is ours all the days of our lives and throughout eternity! Thank you for the greatest gift of all, Lord.

# Evening

Lord, thank you for these angels who come to me in fluff and fur. Thank you for their magic of putting laughter in the hearts of those they love. Thanks for their trust and their unabashed desire to give affection and to be scratched behind the ears.

# Morning

It's easy to go along with what others are doing, and it sometimes feels like the safe thing to do, especially when those "others" are trusted friends. But if we are willing to take a stand for what is right, we can help set a standard for others.

# Evening

What a wonderful day! And now, God of rest and peace, the children are sleeping, replete with the joys of our holiday discoveries that they are savoring to the last drop. We celebrate the joy of ordinary days and rest in your care.

# Morning

Lord, this time of year is a wonderful time for reflecting over the past year. Sometimes there is pain involved in looking back, but there is also so much joy and so many things that fill our hearts with gratitude. Renew our dedication to living a life that brings you glory for as long as we are on this earth. Remind us of the rich heritage that is ours through you, and keep us both humble and grateful.

# Evening

Lord, in your wisdom, you designed us to reject the word "don't." Like all your children, mine do better with "do" words. Do love, share, work, tend, tolerate, obey, forgive. Help me say "do" as often as I can. Let me be a positive example of your vision.

# Morning

Live long enough, and you'll make mistakes. Here's to second chances: at love, at work, in all the machinations of our lives. May we be generous in introducing second chances to others, and may we be open to those granted us. Second chances signify hope.

# Evening

O Lord, how wonderful are your promises! But because I trust your heart more than my own, I only want to receive the desires of my heart if they are desires that originate with you. Teach me to know the difference, Lord—the difference between fleeting, worldly desires and those that have your blessing. Then, Lord—and only then—give me the desires of my heart.

August

# Evening

How easily, O God of eternity, for us to assume our time is like the grains of sand on an ocean beach—vast and endless. Remind us that each of our lives is limited like the sand in the hourglass. May what we do with that sand, play in it, work in it, build our relationships, whatever, be wise use of this precious gift of living.

# Morning

The Lord is my strength and my shield; my heart trusted in him, and I am helped: therefore my heart greatly rejoiceth; and with my song will I praise him.

—Psalm 28:7